HOW TO CREATE
A SUCCESSFUL
COMMERCIAL WEBSITE

FRED COWIE

Straightforward Publishing
www.straightforwardco.co.uk

Straightforward Publishing
Brighton BN2 4EG

ISBN 1903909 65 1

Printed by CATS, Swindon, Wilts

Cover Design by Fred Cowie.

HOW TO CREATE
A SUCCESSFUL
COMMERCIAL WEBSITE

CONTENTS

CONTENTS

CONTENTS

1.

INTRODUCTION

Who is the book aimed at?

First things first – this book is targeted towards those who are involved with small to medium-sized businesses that require a web presence in order to boost their business. It is, therefore, a primer, intended to give a detailed overview of the processes necessary to achieve a successful commercial website. I bring my experience to bear from the view of essential commercial decisions required to put your business firmly into the hub of the web. It is not intended for those businesses involving downloads of software, mp3 (music), videos, etc. as these sites have specific requirements such as hefty servers and "feeds" which require specialised equipment. Also businesses reliant on large database integration will again invariably need costly programmed elements and these are beyond the scope of this book – although the principles of website structure and marketing will still apply.

Throughout the book I attempt to give you a realistic picture of the basic processes involved and warn of the traps into which the unsuspecting can fall – I pull no punches and warn you now that a successful website <u>will</u> incur a considerable on-cost (especially during set-up), on-going maintenance, and regular updates (which provide a dynamic, successful website) must be taken into account. If a business already has experienced IT, sales or marketing personnel, then their skills can be used to alleviate some of the costs. These basic costs will draw on business funds long before you generate the feedback sales, depending, of course, on the effectiveness of your product(s) and marketing. However, it is realistic to look at a number of years, rather than months, to gain a level of traffic through your site giving you some profit. The Internet is a powerful sales medium and is increasingly important to many businesses – although we in Britain have not embraced web shopping as keenly as the USA, it is becoming a stable and trusted medium. Who can afford to ignore the income potential of on-line purchasing?

Essential Building Blocks

The book gives the reader an overview of critical website requirements and options depending on the scope or size of the business. It also attempts to provide a guide to the essential building blocks of how a web site should be constructed (without being too technical) in order to be "search-engine friendly" and integrated into good web promotion. Search engines – like Google or Yahoo – are the indexing systems that allow us to search for web sites – it is vitally important to be friendly to them! The book gives the reader a number of hints and tips – ways to promote your site, cutting down on unnecessary costs, how to avoid web "spammers" who are promising you "amazing" results whilst taking hefty fees for doing very little, and refers to sites that provide useful tools or freebees.

Let's just get a background to the web as it appears today. Since it's inception the internet has gone through a number of incarnations – US Strategic Defence, University Research and Education, Community and Focus Groups, World-Wide Web, Information Highway incorporating multimedia, Commercial showcase/Internet shopping, and with broadband now entrenched, multi-whatever you like!

A New Era

We are entering a new era where all our traditional media is being challenged as never before – we can download music to personal "ipods" and carry around whole jukeboxes of music in a hand-held device. We can hook into digital broadband radio stations from across the world due to clever – nay, very clever - means of compressed digitised sound. We can hook into television broadcasts - admittedly most are recorded in a form of digitised video, but don't blink - TV WILL BE incorporated into web distribution soon on a worldwide scale. We have been conferencing for years, NOW we can videoconference internationally, we can web-phone around the world at local phone charges, we can watch TV on our mobile phones, and this media-integration is going to increase dramatically over the next few years.

A Few Basic Lessons

The web has certainly come a long way since I was teaching computing – I started teaching programming with punched cards (each card equated to a single character!) – equivalent to caveman paintings compared with the web now! So this is our first lesson really – you are dealing with a <u>dynamic environment</u> – it changes almost daily – do not take anything for granted – if this book hasn't been revised in two or so years throw it away! Yes that's how quickly things change on the web – luckily some things do remain more constant than others – and that's what this book is about. Incidentally, I do intend to provide regular revisions to this book! I will not bother you with anything that does not have substance, and will not give you "tricks"(many of these "tricks" are out-dated anyway and may actively compromise your website). I will, instead, focus on you and your business with a long-term approach to creating a web site you will be proud of.

Talking about "tricks" this brings me to the second lesson of web lore – They ARE all out to get you! AND they're good at it! As you surf around the web you will be trapped – like a fly in a spider's web – and find yourself being seduced into all sorts of activities – saving sites as favourites, signing up to newsletters, applying for freebees, etc., etc. Spend some time doing this as an exploratory "game" whilst surfing sites that appeal to you and note <u>HOW you get trapped</u>, succumb to signing-up, etc. Look at the way YOU go for freebees, get seduced by "copy", this is what your site needs – but more of that later. The important thing here is to recognise the difference between legitimate web activity and illegitimate – the web is undergoing a transformation which is being led by search engines – in particular Google (www.Google.com) - which is gradually pushing out all the pornographers, spammers (if you have never had spam emails then you haven't surfed), fraudsters and unsavoury content providers generally.

Lesson number three has got to be – SECURITY – Although the web is probably the last bastion of free speech, and to that extent the global village of the web fraternity put up with EVERYTHING on the web – all the good people who were earnest, honest, and forthright PLUS the religious nutters, loony left activists, right-wing fascists, charlatans, fantasists, hackers, spammers and pornographers – you choose your searches carefully! The web has traditionally been self-policing

– and to that extent it used to get rid of spammers et al by "flaming" (everyone would send thousands of emails to the "spammer" and swamp his system, hey ho - the good ole days – there's too many of 'em now!!! In fact, the web is in danger of becoming swamped by spam emails). In more recent years we have a multiplicity of software protection to shield us from some of these – but make no mistake, the web harbours them all, and anti-virus protection along with firewall protection is a <u>MUST</u>; spyware protection is rapidly becoming a necessity – yes they can invade your computer just by linking to their website – but then business has always had its elements of fraudulent activity and the web lends itself so well to this if you are not careful.

A Few Wise Words

Every silver lining has a cloud! And that brings me neatly to my next point – yes the web is a dynamic environment – yes programmers can do all sorts of wizzy things on the screen but NO you cannot sell that which cannot be sold. You may think that your product(s) is/are the best thing since sliced bread, but if it doesn't sell in a normal retail environment – then why should it sell on the web? This may sound like an obvious statement but you'd be surprised at the number of people who believe that they can start a web business, from scratch, and make a fortune. Remember the "dot-com" revolution! And these were intelligent stock market dealers who normally would check on the necessity of the last penny spent – they were "bamboozled" by the technological dynamism of web progress.

Then there's the moralistic standpoint of Sir Bob Geldorf complaining about the charitable Live8 tickets being sold on ebay, how quickly ebay (www.ebay.com) managed to do something once their reputation was at stake and in the media spotlight – <u>do not underestimate the web</u> – everyone is watching!! Do yourself a favour and keep your feet on the ground – if you can't sell it to your neighbours - you probably can't sell it on the web. Conversely, you can do some things on the web that you can't do on the high street – sometimes you need to think outside the box.

Of course there are exceptions to the rule and the web does attract young entrepreneurs such as those behind "lastminute.com". One of the few "dot-com" successes providing last minute tickets or gifts and organising things such as travel arrangements and concerts – note the web has the edge over ordinary business where speed and efficiency between businesses is concerned. Note also that this service placed itself at the hub of many other successful web ventures and provided a unique selling point - it's "go-getting" users <u>are prepared to pay a premium</u> for the service – this is why it survived!

There are of course also a plethora of smaller businesses that are selling on the web and doing very well at it – those that have achieved success have three things in common – they have planned their web site well, they have unique or competitive products and they have provided for the expense of marketing. Their web sites are therefore dynamic, continually changing and adapting to web-opportunities – their shop window is a changing feast, and surfers will, therefore, return again and again. The silver lining, therefore, does exist and if you are convinced that you have a good product, and have planned well then you CAN market it on the web AND, possibly, make a fortune! The web is global. It <u>can</u> give you incredible coverage – go for it - the sky is the limit.

2.

INITIAL CONSIDERATIONS

Hosted solutions

If your business is small or just starting out you may consider using a web-hosting solution to keep your initial costs down. There are an increasing number of web-hosting services on the web which will enable you to get a web presence quickly, without all the expense of designing and maintaining your own web site, but, unless you are just putting your toe in the internet shopping water, it is the author's opinion that these will not ultimately help your business. The major advantage here is that there are solutions that have virtually no start-up costs and payment can simply be a percentage of the transaction costs – hence you get your money and the provider gets their cut. More sophisticated solutions allow a greater range of controls over the look and feel of your website, BUT, beware of the complexities of the package on offer and read very carefully the small print – there are many who will be all too willing to take your money up-front and leave you struggling to achieve an end result.

Hosting sites that provide you with everything are equivalent to putting your goods in someone else's shop and the host (shop-owner) therefore tends to control your site's look and feel (some have a choice of "templates"), they don't allow your own site name (or, if they do, may not allow you to take it with you if you decide to go your own way – your website name should be registered to you and not the ISP), and often involve the host placing their own advertising links, which take people away from your site. Control is the key – what happens when the host fluffs a transaction? Do you get the blame? How quickly can you change product information? What happens if the host company fails? Now, I'm not trying to be a killjoy, and many of these hosted solutions can provide a relatively cheap way of gaining a web presence, but the main thrust of any advertising that you will be doing is pointing to someone else's domain. They are in control: of the on-screen advertising, of your transactions, of your business! If they put their prices up by 200%, if they put your main rival's products next door, if the site runs slow, etc. what are you going to do? Start again? Having said all this I do recognise that some people will want to look at hosted solutions as a low-cost starting point and I do give more information on these in chapter 5.

Researching the Competition

If you are, however, determined to create your own successful website (and I do recommend this approach) then preparation, research and planning are essential prerequisites. Also knowing what you want your site to look like and what you want to achieve is going to go a long way towards creating a site that is worthy of your business. So – your first task is to surf the web looking for sites that you like, but you must be objective and discerning about the task: keep a log of your preferred sites and list the advantages/disadvantages of each. Someone who is reasonably conversant with surfing the internet and understands the processes involved (your web designer would be good) should be present to point out some of the basic web functionality and to answer your questions. In the process you will want to look carefully at sites that are your direct competitors – you will probably realise fairly quickly which of these are the most successful (the first that you come upon on search engines usually) – try to use more than one search engine when doing your research e.g. Google and Yahoo (the top two most popular).

Find Unique Selling Points

During your research note what makes competitor sites attractive and popular – not that you want your site to look the same, you don't, BUT you <u>do</u> want to emulate the essential attractions. This analysing process should not be totally objective (what attracts can be very subjective) and the best way to proceed is to meet with your directors or fellow workers to discuss the relative merits/demerits of each site and, if possible, find unique elements of your own business or products that the other sites don't have. I cannot stress too much what unique selling points will do to enhance your site above others – this is vitally important and we will come back to this point later.

The Importance of Links

Another major research area to look for are "outbound links" (links [adverts] to other sites from each site you're analysing) – these are often to associated (or affiliated) businesses, or suppliers to the business, and if you follow these you will invariably find that there are links back (inbound links back to the original site). This mutual (or reciprocal) linking serves to enhance "web profile" i.e. the more sites you link to giving reciprocal links back give more routes for web surfers to find your site – this is increasingly important for a successful web site.

The Importance of Copy

The whole look and feel of your web site is vitally important – and a competent person should be chosen to write the required "copy". By copy I mean the words used on your site to describe your products and to attract potential customers – and this is not as easy as some may think! You may decide to undertake this task in conjunction with your own sales/marketing staff and the web designer in the initial specification stage – your sales staff understand the unique selling points of your products and the web designer will understand the ways in which web surfers click-through navigation links and this is crucial to creating a good web site. As you surf from site to site on the web you are instinctively guided to ways of gaining information, narrowing down searches, getting sidetracked and resorting to instinct for avoiding irrelevant adverts and links.

Look and Feel

All sites provide a look and feel according to their target audience – a site selling toys will probably give an air of excitement and entertainment with bright primary colours, whereas a site selling computer components will provide an air of being up-to-date with the latest gadgets and technical info, offer various deals and fast delivery, etc. The point being, the "copy" will be totally different according to the target audience. The copy should immediately show clients what to expect as they get deeper into the website – the first page or screen should portray quickly what the site is about and what it is selling – give information or deals or discounts on the most popular products – and give access to categories/subcategories of products for ease of access. The whole tone of your copy should guide the surfer to what they are looking for without insulting their intelligence or putting them off in any way. The copy must entice, explain, and direct people, but also allow them to browse through the virtual shop easily – consider a "site map" if your site is large or in any way complicated.

"Langauge, spelling, and ability of the copyrighter is vitaly important!" Sorry about the above sentence but see what I mean – apart from appalling spelling did you spot that it should read "are vitally important"!! Poor spelling or grammar immediately deters the reader from continuing – mistakes or waffle reflect badly on the professionalism of your site and surfers will be quickly looking for the "Back" button. Your copy must be informative with good headings, subheadings, layout, images, easy to use links and navigation etc. The copy is also what search-engines use to index and categorise your site, which is why there's plenty of discussion about "website optimisation", "keywords", "page ranking", etc. on the web.

What does a Search-Engine actually do?

The search engine (e.g. Google is found at www.google.com) is a complicated beast BUT it is the most common way most people will arrive at a site and is therefore vitally important. It is an essential tool on the web and why there are so many of them. Essentially what they do is take the "copy" from your site's web-page and sift through it ignoring the HTML(web-page language) and minor words ("and", "but", etc) and indexing what they consider to be key words and phrases along with your website description (usually from your web-page's HTML Meta Description tag) and your URL (your site's name). For instance, if your site sells lawn-mowers and the words "lawn-mower" or "mower" are mentioned several times within the copy, then the search engine determines that this is a significant "keyword" and will index your site amongst all the other 'lawn-mower' sites in their database – in theory! If your web page, however, tries to be smart and your copy merely states:-

> "lawn-mowers, lawnmowers, mowers, affordable mowers, discounted lawnmowers, l a w n m o w e r s, etc."

this is considered to be "spamming" (i.e. repetition of keywords in order to improve your search ranking – not to be confused with unsolicited emails) and the search-engine may demote your site or worse, these days, ban it altogether from their database!

Keywords and Copy

There are many ways that search engines categorise keywords and each engine has changed over the years in order to serve up a good result to the person searching its database. Your web-pages are ranked according to things such as keyword placement, keyword prominence, keyword frequency, etc. and points are awarded according to the relevance that the search-engine gives to these scores affecting where your site comes in their search results. The problem is that this process is getting more and more complex, and the way in which different search engines do this, increasingly difficult to determine. The point being that – whilst it is important to structure your web-pages well, and have good, informative copy that search-engines will index well, don't let anyone tell you that they can increase <u>significantly</u> your search rankings, page relevance, etc., through "page optimisation". Search-engine optimisation is, these days, more of an art-form than a scientific methodology and, lets be honest, not everyone is going to achieve top-ranking results with the massively increasing number of sites coming onto the web each year.

Search-Engine Methods are Constantly Changing

Search-engines are becoming increasingly more sophisticated – notable amongst the many is of course the amazing rise to fame of "Google". This company came from nowhere to being the most used search-engine on the planet – why? Well, a number of reasons really, but essentially it took the search-engine from a flat, straightforward indexing system to a sophisticated language-driven relational database providing, amongst other things, contextual relationships. Well – you did ask! This is similar in many ways to the word processors that give us grammar-checking and thesaurus; complex language deconstruction and word association techniques.

What does this mean for our website? Well, it means that every other major search-engine had to do a lot of catching up and Google claims to have something like 35%-40% of the search-engine market, with Yahoo and its owned subsidiaries of Altavista, AllTheWeb and Overture at about 25%-30%. It also means that many of the things that web designers and webmasters were doing in the past to get their site ranking well was ignored by Google – it used a whole new algorithmic sophistication of methods to produce better search results. It also rejected sites that used various dubious methods of gaining false rankings like "spamming", "hidden (spamming) text", "link farms", and other such wonders of website wizardry!

Search-Engine Optimisation

There are many sites to advise you on "search-engine optimisation" (SEO's are in the business of getting your website higher up the search lists), and whilst they will purport to give you hints and tips to improve your search results, they will make it seem incredibly complicated and suggest that they will do it all for you - at a price of course! However, common sense will tell you to provide some uniqueness of words in your web page copy that the search-engines will index – they index phrases or groups of words as well as just single keywords. For instance, say you are selling a particular lawn mower – then, rather than saying:-

> "The latest lawn-mower from the well-known manufacturer 'Riley', called the 'Suffolk Punch', rolls and spikes your lawn, at the same time, increasing aeration", use
>
> "The 'Riley Suffolk Punch' lawnmowers uniquely roll and spike your lawn".

Not only is the second sentence more compact, it contains a unique label of keywords for the product – by putting the words "Riley" and "Suffolk" and "Punch" and "lawnmowers" together, anyone searching for this product (by using a combination of search words e.g. "Riley lawnmowers" or "Suffolk Punch mower") will find the site before looking through the search results at sites about the "Suffolk" county or before recipes for "punch" drinks or before sites about "Suffolk Punch" horses! Not magic – just common sense and an understanding of how search-engines work. It is better also to work on combinations of words or phrases – try putting yourself in the mind of the surfer and think what words they would use in finding your site – for instance anyone looking for lawn-mowers might be looking first for information to help them choose, so, the words "choosing a lawn-mower" would be a good phrase to use in your copy. Using brand names will give you more unique search results – think about the name "Flymo"™, for instance, it is instantly recognisable as a form of hover mower and is absolutely unique to the manufacturer, and more importantly, the word has no other meaning in the dictionary. However, there will of course be other websites selling these mowers so again think of how the surfer will find your site – again, 'choosing a Flymo' might be good, or 'Flymo review' or 'the best Flymo distributor in ……' should all be considered.

The Rise of Contextual Advertising

Google also developed a set of advertising methods that gave value for money over the old "Banner Ads" and "Pay-per-Click" type of marketing. Google's "Adwords" for instance, allow the client to put a cap on how much his advert costs per month but still gets prime-placed contextual ranking (e.g. a search on "grass care" might bring in an advert for lawnmowers) and thus guides a set level of potential buyers to his site. It gives the client control of his advertising and Google guarantee a level of service and advice to help the client. This is a long way from the old banner ads. and pay-per-click regime where the marketing company controlled the budget and you couldn't be sure of what you were paying for. Some disreputable companies were known to employ a network of surfers to jump back and forth onto banner ads, etc. and therefore give the false impression that a site was popular – you get no sales and the company gets your advertising revenue – great eh! Then they developed automated programs to emulate a surfer to do the job for them! (Check out this hijacking story -

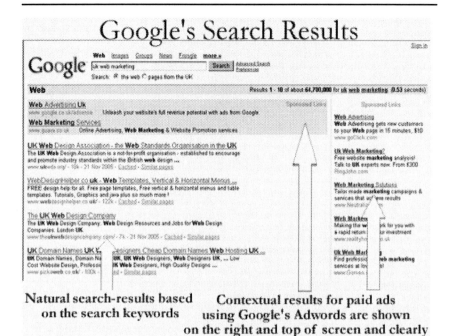

Natural search-results based on the search keywords

Contextual results for paid ads using Google's Adwords are shown on the right and top of screen and clearly marked as 'Sponsored Links'

http://www.lurhq.com/ppc-hijack.html). This sort of behaviour is thankfully becoming less, but it is always possible given the anonymity that the web can provide – it is well to always keep your guard up and check out any services on the web before parting with your money. Sad but true.

Google has made a good start in avoiding many of the scammers and recently embarked on the amazingly immense task of scanning every, yes every, page of every book (English language only) published and in libraries, in the world!!! It expects to have achieved this amazing feat within six years – and from then on it will be the biggest on-line repository ever. There is a price to pay for being the number one search-engine – but Google has managed to create a huge business opportunity for itself by consistently being one step ahead. What this means for you and your website is that you need to look at Google's advertising opportunities very closely, and consider using these to boost your web-presence.

3.

ESSENTIAL ELEMENTS OF A WEBSITE

All successful websites have essential elements that, whilst they are common to many, need to be implemented with professionalism and skill in order to give the user the best possible experience.

These elements are:

❑ Home Page - An attractive and informative home page that immediately gives the user an overall understanding of what your site is about. The first page a user enters, normally, called 'index.html' and is the entry point to your whole site. This opening page should give clear indications of the main navigation routes to further pages and make the user feel secure and interested in going further to find more information.

❑ Who You Are - Basic company information should be available from any page on your site – again this is to give the user security that you are who you say you are, and that they can contact you either by email or phone if necessary. It is all about building customer confidence in your site and your products. Furthermore your site should have further assurances to customers in the form of a statement of company ethics and terms of reference regarding their rights in trading over the internet (for government guidelines see www.dti.gov.uk/ccp/topics1/ecomm.htm).

❑ Clear and Easy to Use - The products being offered should have informative (rather than hyped) descriptions and include where appropriate images (photographs in jpeg format) with clear specifications (item reference numbers, sizes, etc.) and pricing information. Normally you would also include a button which allows inclusion in your "shopping trolley" and initiating an on-line purchase of the item. The process of on-line purchasing should be a simple and straightforward process where the customer can see that their credit card is acceptable and can complete the process easily on secure servers. The process should provide for an email notification that thanks them and confirms their purchase with a unique purchase (tracking) number in case of delivery problems. There may be cases where you prefer to allow the customer to simply give their contact information – for instance, if you are selling very high-priced goods or technically complex items that would need a more direct contact with the customer.

❑ Easily Downloaded Information - An on-line catalogue of your products should be easily available for download – again you are trying to be professional and allow the user to peruse your products in a printed form. Perhaps they want to discuss purchase with a colleague or partner at a later date. Obviously you must make every effort to maintain this catalogue in line with any item or price changes – although this can be a chore, always think of the customer's point of view -

they may have spent ages deciding on a product you no longer stock! The standard way of presenting this catalogue is in "pdf"(Adobe Acrobat – a web-printer-friendly file) format and you should always attempt to keep the size of the catalogue as small as possible for fast download times. Although Adobe Acrobat is the most prominent software allowing this type of universal (PC's, Mac's, etc) download I have found that providing an alternative "Word" (Microsoft) version is as popular and often provides smaller file sizes. When offering downloads always give a file-size indication to the user – those on slower dial-up systems can get worried/angry if their system is locked up doing a long download and are just as likely to switch off – both their systems and your site!

❑ Customer Focus - Customer feedback is an important part of any site – this could be a simple request for information on a product, taking up an offer that you are promoting, or a request for update information in the future. This is normally in the shape of an on-line "form" that the user fills in – keep it simple and quick for the user – anything more than email address, phone number, name and address, and a couple of choices/tick-boxes, etc. can be off-putting. Also remember this is personal and private information the user is giving you – it MUST be protected in an inaccessible (to outsiders) file on your site and you cannot use this information other than for the purposes that you have given (Data Protection Act). Most importantly, you must ensure that you follow up the users request promptly and efficiently – internet users (quite rightly) expect this and you want your business to have a good reputation.

❑ FAQ's - (Frequently Asked Questions) – A common feature of websites that, again, builds confidence in the user by attempting to pre-empt their queries. Normally the best way to present these is on a separate page with a list of questions in descending order of popularity. The user clicks on the link question and is taken to the area on the page giving the answer. Questions about payment over the internet, delivery of goods, and their basic rights if not satisfied are prime questions to be at the top of the list. FAQ's should be a dynamic feedback page – your customer services should be keeping track of customers queries and making sure that the most common ones or those about your latest product line are fed back to this page – the internet, if nothing else, should always provide good information.

❑ Building a Web Presence - Articles, reviews and press releases are another element of successful sites and, at the risk of repeating myself, again build confidence in the user. By including these, with links to other sites where these reviews are seen to be endorsing your products, you are showing that your products are universally accepted. If you can further your site by contacting sites that specialise in reviews and establish reciprocal links you will be enhancing your web profile – and the top search engines are now putting a heavy emphasis on this "link popularity" in ranking websites (is there a difference between link-popularity and link-farming? Try searching on 'Search-engine link popularity').

Choose a Good Internet Service Provider

Another important consideration in the planning of your site is choosing an ISP (Internet Service Provider): The ISP can prove critical to the operation of your site – it is a choice that needs some research although your website designer may be able to help you here and give recommendations. The point here is that not all ISP's offer the same range of functionality and it depends on your web site requirements as to whether some of the things you may want to do are possible. Firstly, let me warn you against attempting to do this cheaply – there are ISP's who offer "free" web space and, as with many of the so-called "freebies", they come with limitations or restrictions – some you only find out about when certain web functionality doesn't work or additional functionality requires payment!

There is also the added drawback of "guilt by association" where some search engines will severely limit the indexing of certain ISP's because they contain too many junk or half-baked experimental sites – your site is not taken seriously. A serious business ought to be prepared to pay for a recognised commercial ISP – you can find recommendations at this ISP review site, which also has some good advice on choosing ISP's (http://www.ispreview.co.uk/articles/choose/). Many ISP's provide a service such that they will organise the provision of your domain name (the world-wide web name that you want to call your site) and this can make things a lot simpler for you.

There are sites that allow you to check whether certain domain names already exist (try www.allwhois.com which returns the owners identity and location) – obviously, choosing your name is important. Your domain name should ideally reflect your current company name, but this is not always possible – there is a whole plethora of domain-name businesses that grew rapidly in the eighties when people realised that companies would pay a lot to have certain obvious company names and duly registered everything that was potentially lucrative (similar to number-plate collectors). Since then there have been a number of legal cases going against this practice where certain companies took exception to having their registered company names hijacked in this way (in fact, many names become available every year because those who own them don't keep up the payments). So if you want to use your company name and this has already been registered by someone who is merely a collector of names (i.e. it's been hijacked) then you may still be able to recover the use of that name, either through legal means or by paying for it. This can be a complex area, crossing as it does international boundaries, and it is often less trouble to think up another adaptation of your trading name.

The Importance of Your Website Name

So, how important is a website name? The answer is, of course, very important – your website name should be easily remembered to be most effective. Generally it should be ideally short and descriptive; take for example www.bbc.co.uk, everyone in the UK knows instantly what this company is and what it does. OK, you might say, well that's obvious because the company has been around for so long and www.britbroadcastco.co.uk or something like would be too clumsy and difficult – yes exactly. Take our previous lawnmower example, we could choose www.wilsons.co.uk - it's short but there are probably many other companies called Wilsons and it doesn't actually give us a clue what the company is about, whereas. www.wilsons-mowers.co.uk, does

– it tells us the company name, what they do, <u>and</u> is easily remembered. You could actually make up any name at all, such as www.wilmow.co.uk, but although it's short is still not as easily remembered or as obvious as the previous suggestion. You can't always get what you want, however, and some names that you think up will already, legitimately, have been taken – but avoid complication if you can. It may be useful to know that if you are a registered UK limited company then you can use yourbusinessname.ltd.uk or yourbusinessname.plc.uk, which are reserved for this purpose.

ISP Capacity and Facilities

Not all ISP's are the same, and choosing the right one for your needs depends, very much, on what your website requirements are in terms of bandwidth, size, facilities, reliability, etc. For example, "POBOXinternet" which claims to be "The UK's oldest independent ISP", details its basic services as in the diagram shown. Running through these options:

  ❑Bandwidth allowance refers to the number of people who can comfortably access your site without any degradation in speed of browsing.

  ❑Free UK Domain Registration is obviously self-explanatory and a bonus.

  ❑Mysql Database is a common and sophisticated database available to a number of web applications.

  ❑FrontPage extensions refer to Microsoft's "Frontpage" web-design package and would be a distinct advantage if your site is using this application.

	Hosting Plus	Hosting 50	Hosting 250**
Bandwidth Allowance*	10Gb	50Gb	250Gb
Free .uk Domain Reg	Yes	Yes	Yes
Mysql Database	Yes	Yes	Yes
Front Page Extensions	[Windows]	[Windows]	No
PHP Support	[icon]	[icon]	Yes
ASP Support	[Windows]	[Windows]	No
ASP.NET Support	[Windows]	[Windows]	No
Web Space	Unlimited	Unlimited	Unlimited
Mail Boxes	Unlimited	Unlimited	Unlimited
.NET Support	[Windows]	[Windows]	No
Built In Web Stats	Yes	Yes	Yes
SSL	Yes	Yes	Yes
Monthly	£8	£25	£30
	Buy Now	Buy Now	Buy Now

- PHP Support is support of "Pre-Hypertext Processor", a widely used HTML-embedded scripting language often used in conjunction with Mysql Database.
- ASP Support is support for Microsoft's Active Server Pages software which delivers web-pages dynamically, a scripting language enabling creation of web pages "on the fly", i.e. programmed according to responses of the surfer.
- ASP.NET Support - Microsoft's Web servers (note this support disappears on the highest bandwidth?)
- Web space and mailbox space is unlimited, which is nice – some ISP's will charge you above a certain amount of space used.
- .NET support - Microsoft again (note this support disappears on the highest bandwidth?)

❑Built-in web stats - refers to visitor statistics which can provide you with essential marketing information.

❑SSL is "secure socket layer" security that allows you to keep captured information in a ciphered code and immune from theft – this facility is often a pricey add-on.

So we can see that this looks fairly robust in terms of facilities offered on a typically commercial ISP. However, if our web-designer, for example, prefers to use a database system known as Coldfusion Mark-up Language (CFML), then we might be in trouble here as the ISP doesn't appear to support it within the basic package. It is therefore vitally important that the choice of the ISP depends on your website requirements, and you must discuss these <u>fully</u> with your web-designer <u>before</u> you select your ISP.

4.

STAFFING YOUR WEBSITE

An important part of your planning must be the staff you choose to create and manage your web site. These staff must be capable of managing your site, ensuring security and smooth operations, as well as responding to customer queries, orders, and fulfilment of orders. You must, at least, appoint:- a webmaster, a website designer, and a customer liaison/order fulfilment operator. Other operators can be added as orders grow, but these positions are absolutely necessary.

Webmaster

The webmaster is the person with overall responsibility for the technical side of operating a live web site – they are responsible for communications with your ISP, the security and operations of the web site, and general trouble-shooter of technical problems. The webmaster is the central point of communications regarding all aspects of web-management and control - the person responsible should be able to move quickly and efficiently where problems arise. This position may be within the capabilities of your internal computer expert or you may prefer to contract this out to your web design company – although you must remember that they may be providing this service for a number of clients and therefore you must be sure of the level of response that they are promising.

Website Designer

The website designer is normally contracted, preferably locally, and is responsible for overall design – look and feel – of your site as well as being capable of offering a range of operational choices for communications to and from your site to your order/fulfilment department, etc. Although many computer programmer/analysts are capable of understanding the workings of a web site – and capable of using software packages such as Dreamweaver or Frontpage ("what-you-see-is-what-you-get" web design packages) – don't make the mistake that you could get your internal computer "expert" to do all the work themselves! Good programmers are not traditionally the best graphics designers and you may be stretching their expertise to the limit. You may know of a friend who will tell you it's easy and you don't have to pay a professional – be very wary, unless they can provide adequate proof of working sites that you can verify as being their own work! It is far better to outsource this work to those who are doing it all the time – they will give you a far better service, without delays or errors, and provide you with a soundly designed web site that makes use of the latest technological innovations.

Who Owns Your Website?

In choosing your designer make sure that you follow basic sound business practice of selecting a short-list and follow-up by seeking recommendations from some of their clients – it is my view that your designer should be local and easily available (cheap web design offers on the web may be tempting, but if they are in the outback of Australia and don't perform what can you do if anything goes wrong?). Contractual arrangements with your web designer should be looked at carefully and you should ensure that you retain the copyright of the final web site code produced – some web designers will retain copyright and attempt to keep control of a lucrative maintenance agreement where no other person will be able to alter or change 'their' design. Of course, one has to be reasonable here, as a good web designer will be proud of their work and want to be acknowledged for this – what they don't want is someone else altering what is essentially their work and then be blamed for non-functionality of the site – this involves some discussion but stick to your guns in terms of future-proofing your investment. If you retain copyright then you may be paying a bit more, but you are in control - if your web designer is not providing a good service, etc. then you can switch designer and your site can continue to grow. Most web designers should be pleased to give you a number of sites that they have designed – some of these may however be "friendly" clients who are getting preferred rates for providing recommendations – so be careful - it is wise to get an initial specification and quote for the work required.

You may decide that your IT "expert" is capable of providing regular updates to the site once they have a "template" to work on – this is perfectly feasible, especially if they can be backed up through a support contract with your original web designer.

Processing Your Orders

A fulfilment or order-processing person will be required to control the whole processing of orders from the web site. The complexity of this position depends on the number and extent of sales through the web site: small numbers of distinct items being relatively easy to control, however, a site selling a large range of component parts will probably need more complex tracking procedures. These can normally be controlled by downloading orders into a database, such as Microsoft's "Access", or into a spreadsheet like "Excel", and having procedures to record orders and provide transaction logging (really complex operations will need to get specific stock-control/order-processing software and will consequently be looking at a high computer on-cost). An important task would be the ability to pre-empt changes to web site prices, discounts, discontinued or new stock lines, in conjunction with the webmaster to implement the changes.

Customer Liaison

Customer liaison is another vital role – and the internet is unremitting where poor service is concerned. A customer service position could well be integrated into the order fulfilment role at first – if the number of orders is moderately low. The main responsibility is to answer email messages coming in from the website or sent through the normal email traffic to the company on a regular basis. Ask yourself how long you would be prepared to wait for a reply to an enquiry about a product you wanted to buy? The ideal situation being that these incoming emails should alert the operator and answers should be virtually immediate – anything less than this could lose you customers.

They must also be prepared to field all sorts of enquiries about the products, the means of transaction processing, the delivery times, etc. This service should be quick and easy to implement – web shoppers expect to get quick service – that's the name of the game – if they don't (and there is never a good excuse) then they will be off elsewhere in a click. An important feedback of this service is for the operator to communicate any problems to the webmaster and provide useful information, such as extra FAQ's (Frequently Asked Questions), product descriptions, articles/reviews of products, etc. for inclusion on the web site. Your website therefore remains dynamic and provides answers to your customers at the point of origin.

Finally, your staff must be well educated – they must understand what they are doing, why they are doing it and how to do it. Your website designer might be helpful here with the required training – but if your staff are not capable of dealing with all situations then it's your business that will suffer.

5.

SHOPPING TROLLEYS AND E-COMMERCE

Now this is where things can get complicated, and there are many types of e-commerce solution providers on the web, all of whom want to convince you that their own solution is the best – and of course, that you deserve the best, and should be prepared to pay through the nose for it! Don't forget that the web does have some dubious companies who are prepared to offer you a poor service but are always willing to take your money up front.

Partially-Hosted solutions

It is always wise to be cautious and many reputable software vendors are now tending to allow you to try their packages out first – so look for these opportunities and take advantage of them in order to be sure of what you are purchasing. It is also wise not to assume anything, read carefully any contractual obligations and ask for a complete breakdown of expected pricing. For reasons that I have already mentioned I am assuming that, at this point, you have decided to have your own domain name which is running on your chosen ISP's servers. This already excludes many totally hosted solutions (where your website is totally in the control of a third-party provider) but still leaves us with a plethora of partially-hosted solutions (these 'hosts' are sometimes known as application service providers (i.e. providing applications such as shopping-trolley and/or order-processing software).

E-Commerce Banking Process

In order to outline the range of solutions we need to understand the basic e-commerce payment cycle that underlies all shopping-trolley applications.

- ❑ A customer to your site is enabled via some shopping-trolley software to place an order for your goods using their credit card.
- ❑ This order is normally transmitted in encrypted code, called secure socket layers (SSL), to your acquiring bank, which is where you have a merchant account.
- ❑ This process immediately goes through the credit-card network (inter-bank security) to the customers card-issuing bank, for clearance that the funds are available and approved.
- ❑ An approval (or denial) is then sent immediately back to your acquiring bank(your merchant account) and they return this to you as an acceptance or denial of funds.
- ❑ You get the order normally as an email giving you transaction details and can organise the shipping of the order – in theory – in practice, this step often takes place <u>after</u> the final transfer of funds.
- ❑ You then request your funds for the order from your merchant account.
- ❑ This generates a request for funds from the issuing bank's customer account and thus completes the authorised payment to your merchant account. This is often referred to as 'capture of funds' and banks are now insisting that all internet purchases (card not present transactions) are actually flagged as such due to increasing levels of fraud.

❏ However, even though the transaction is authorised it may still take two or three days for the funds to actually appear in your merchant account! Yes, bank computers are slow when it comes to paying out!

Ok – got that – and all this happens in a twinkling of your bank manager's eye! Yes, it appears to be overcomplicated – but unless you are prepared to use other means of payment – such as "Paypal" (ebay's own "person to person payment" mechanism which is, if anything, more complicated) – then you are stuck with it I'm afraid.

Credit Cards

People are usually quite happy about paying by credit-card as long as your website conveys a good level of confidence to them – assuring them of their rights and that you are a responsible company is half the battle. You must be aware of your responsibilities when selling goods over the web – the laws are similar to mail-order purchases and you are bound to supply goods on-time, and complete transactions within the law – see the governments website (http://www.dti.gov.uk/ccp/topics1/ecomm.htm).

Delivery and Refunds

If, for some reason, you can't supply the goods, or worse - some of the goods on the order, then the above credit-payment process, or part of it, may have to be reversed or supplemented by a balancing transaction!!! Your merchant account is normally capable of doing all this and you will have on-line access to it – the question is – is your shopping trolley software capable of facilitating and keeping track of it? This is the big question – and the answer is anything but clear – there is a difference between shopping trolleys and comprehensive order-processing software, which will be able to handle more complex problems like returned goods, partial fulfilment, back orders, etc. – the answer is, therefore, generally linked to "how much are you willing to pay?" – no surprises there then!

Other payment methods

E-commerce is in fact a lot less complicated (believe it or not) than it used to be – and competition has served to simplify the whole process of setting up your own merchant account. There is nothing wrong with asking for a cheque, although this is not really as instant as the internet is expected to be, and this inevitably restricts delivery until the cheque clears. Then there is "Paypal" - which is a no-fee – no start up cost, alternative person to person payment system. I myself have always steered clear, as they are intrinsically associated with ebay-type auction transactions. There are sites such as www.ebay-sucks.com which are full of disgruntled (ripped-off?) people, and this doesn't tend to engender confidence in your own customers. I realise that this is guilt by association, but on the web you cannot afford bad publicity – you certainly don't want to court it. (Last minute note - Interestingly, I have just checked the ebay-sucks site again and it has changed completely from about 3 months ago – it is now not an angry site at all and has cute references to ebay – I wonder who took over?).

Internet Merchant Accounts

I also tend to only go with UK banks for internet merchant accounts; again, not that I don't trust others, it's just that if there are problems you can actually pin someone down without going on a long-haul flight! Also fees and facilities vary considerably, as do competence, and I have elected in the past to go with "Worldpay" (www.worldpay.com - a division of the Royal Bank of Scotland), who maintain a reasonably low-cost set-up and provide an efficient and personable service. At the risk of repeating myself UK banks vary considerably in their charges (and ability!) to set-up a merchant account – beware!

Shopping Trolley Software

Your shopping trolley software can be facilitated in a number of ways:-

i)   It could be part of a complete order-processing package which runs on your website totally under your control, except for the actual e-commerce interface to your merchant account.

ii)   It could be part of a complete order-processing package which runs either on your website or on the hosts' servers, but is under the control of the host-owners of the software, who are effectively renting it to you, and who also control the interface to your merchant account. These solutions are often partnered with particular banks and you have little choice. – beware the merchant account charges!

iii)   It could be a partially hosted package that runs shopping trolley software only on the host computer and allows interfaces with your merchant account from there.

The above are not exact choices and are given as an illustration of the range of shopping-trolley software available – in truth you can find software which combine any elements of the above.

Complete Order Processing Software

The first option is suitable for companies selling a large or complicated range of products and expect a huge web sales turnover. It has the advantage of being totally under your control (or more explicitly the control of your web-designer/programmer!), but this is a double-edged sword, as order-processing can be a complicated process and internet security issues alone mean that there could be costly updates, to plug security holes for instance, on a regular basis. Your web-designer may or may not be capable of this, as it involves heavy programming work requiring special skills and experience (which never comes cheap) and they may need to call in expensive programmers.

However, there are packages available which give you a complete order-processing system incorporated into database functionality and which have such capabilities as order-processing, back-orders, stock-control, etc. Some of these are backed by big-named companies, such as Microsoft's 'Commerce Manager', but don't be fooled into thinking they will cater for all your needs – you must still check the level of functionality! There are packages that are available free or relatively cheap, which give a decent level of functionality and can be upgraded to suit your own requirements by an experienced programmer – (try searching on 'web order processing shareware'), but remain wary when evaluating these and try before you buy – if possible. The programming of these packages requires a high level of experienced personnel as website functionality remains varied, complex and fraught with security problems - in particular, many packages are specifically designed for US companies. If your orders are likely to be complex and contain multiple-products, multiple-lines, complicated pricing structures, etc., and there is a need to combine partial-fulfilment of orders as well as generating back-orders or stock-control, raising purchase orders, etc., or if you expect a high level of returns then this approach is going to get very complicated and costly, <u>unless you have chosen your software carefully</u> and it does everything that you want.

Order-Processing from an Application Service Provider

The second option is a viable option for the medium-sized business, as it combines the skills of your web-designer with the skills, and efficiency, of a major developer of order-processing software. Often this option is partially hosted meaning that the software controlling your order processing is actually resident on a completely different server somewhere else in the world! This may seem strange but is a common occurrence on the internet and the whole process appears seamless to your customers. The software will handle the actual shopping trolley processing, but further allows for such niceties as fulfilment tracking, partial-order fulfilment, back-orders, etc. It will also provide you with various reporting options showing sales figures, most popular products, etc. Although you will be paying an overhead for the "rental" or leasing of the software you are not responsible for the maintenance or updating of a complex application package. It gives you the flexibility of a comprehensive order-processing package without needing the services of expensive programmers. Again, you must choose the package carefully and be convinced that it serves all your needs.

A Simple Partially-Hosted Shopping Trolley

The third option is one which is suitable for a small to medium-sized business where the number of products being sold isn't excessive – this will be the most popular approach for those just starting a fairly straightforward web-presence. The shopping trolley can be hosted by a third-party on their own servers and is normally configurable as to colour, headings, discounts, shipping fees, currency, etc. so that it maintains the look and feel of the rest of your website.

Furthermore, it allows interfacing to a merchant account for credit card processing – ideally this doesn't restrict you to just one bank or merchant account option, i.e. you are not tied-in and can switch to another merchant account if required. This option doesn't give you all the software needed for complete order-processing – it does process your orders, it takes care of payment, and gives you transaction details but leaves it up to you to organise your own records as to order-fulfilment, partial-fulfilment, stock-control, etc. Some of these allow you to download order transactions as computer-friendly files, which allows them to be incorporated into a database on your office computer so that you can maintain your own order-processing – either on a relatively simple basis or integrated into a standard order-processing software package.

The Magic Buy Button

Most of these hosted options rely on the links attached to the "Buy" button next to the product. For instance, on the Straightforward publisher's website the button illustrated:

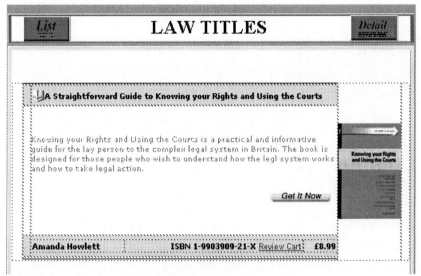

The "Buy" button, (which actually says "Get It Now"), has a link attached to it as detailed below:

```
<a
href="http://ww8.aitsafe.com/cf/add.cfm?userid=A480006&
product=Knowing+Your+Rights+and+Using+the+Courts&
price=8.99&return=www.straightforwardco.co.uk/law_books.
html"><img src="images/getitnow.gif" width="82"
height="21" border="0"></a>
```

The first part of the link is whisking you away to the service vendors (Mals e-commerce website – www.mals-e.com) website named "ww8.aitsafe.com" and showing you a shopping trolley page with your intended purchase – more specifically it goes to a subdirectory called "cf" (customer functions?) and an item called "add.cfm" which is a function or program on that site adding this item to the shopping trolley. The information following the question mark contains unique information to the shopping trolley software about the product being ordered. The "userid" denotes that this information is coming from the Straightforward Publishing website, the "product" is the name of the book (product) and uses "+" signs which are changed to spaces in the shopping trolley, the "price" is the product price, and the "return" is the web-page address to which the shopping trolley will return after displaying the items in the trolley so far.

Basically, once you are on this shopping trolley page you can then elect to "continue" to the payment page and give your name and address and credit card details to complete the transaction. All of this takes place on the solution vendor's site and this site should have 'secure socket layers' (SSL - often denoted in your browser by a little key symbol) which ciphers your information and keeps it from prying eyes.

Interfacing with your Merchant Account

The shopping trolley software will then interface with your chosen acquiring bank's merchant account to get authorisation and complete the process. Now, you don't want to have to go through all this security to then transfer these details over an unsecured e-mail, so the transaction details are normally held on the secure site only, and although you may get notification of the order by e-mail (which just gives a transaction id with no credit-card details) it is then up to you to log onto the secure site with your allocated password to get this customers address and order information for order fulfilment.

Advantages of Hosted Shopping Trolleys

This "hosted" shopping trolley therefore has a number of advantages for the small business:-

❑ Your web designer simply has to concentrate on design – it is easy for the designer to add 'buy' buttons with the accompanying links to the hosted shopping trolley as shown previously.

❑ You don't have to worry about security of customer information as it is being taken care of by the host.

❑ You pay a comparatively small fee for the use of the shopping trolley software (Mals fees for a premium account are £10 per quarter or £36.00 per annum) and as long as there are options of integrating into more than one payment gateway, you keep your options open as to which bank gives you a good merchant account service. (A Worldpay merchant account set-up and fees for a year are probably less than £400 for a small website). The big advantage here is that the host maintains all the difficult programming required for access to the payment gateways/merchant accounts.

❑ You have easy access to the shopping trolley configuration set-up and can set your discount structures, postage, packing and shipping structures as well as setting up your own headings, footers, change colours, add logos, etc. depending on the flexibility of the shopping trolley. I must add here that although I researched Mal's shopping trolley thoroughly, and tested it before buying, it may not suit everyone – you must check that the software will give you the flexibility that you require for your products, your discounts, your post and packing costs, etc. A further problem actually arose with Worldpay as they have a restriction that any transaction must be £10.00 or more, and some books being sold on the Straightforward site were, even with added postage, coming under this restriction. This was easily solved by raising the prices on a small number of books.

Disadvantages of Hosted Shopping Trolleys

The disadvantages of the hosted shopping trolley are:-

❑ The simple shopping trolley is good for small to medium volumes of sales, but if you have high volumes, and consequently a large number of returned goods, or back-orders, partial fulfilment, etc. then keeping track of everything might prove a problem.

❑ Some shopping trolleys give a level of integration into office accounting systems by allowing for download of database-friendly files from your order transactions, otherwise you are in a situation where you are manually fulfilling your orders and manually updating your accounting systems to keep in line with internet sales.

❑ You don't have total control over the actions of the host – if they provide a poor service, if their servers are always closing down for maintenance, etc. then your business will suffer.

❑   There are often no ways of catering for VAT in the shopping trolley software and this is largely due to the complexities of catering for international tax considerations in general. The easy answer is to simply give your prices inclusive of VAT – however, this may not please your accounts department who will have to disentangle the VAT element of sales.

In general, it is beneficial for a small to medium-sized company to take a partially hosted simple shopping-trolley option, in terms that much of the security risk and functionality is taken care of by the host-owner of the software. This leaves the web-designer to take on a fairly straightforward role of maintaining and updating the essential marketing thrust of your site. If your website becomes busy and causes complications with fulfilment of orders then you can easily switch to a more comprehensive order-processing supported hosting package and although you may be paying more for the extra functionality of the software – you are avoiding heavy programming costs that would otherwise start to bite into the profitability of your site.

All the hosted solutions rely on a similar method of linking from the "Buy" button, and its associated link-attributes, as already illustrated. It is therefore easy for your web-designer to go through these links and change them to point at a new, hosted package that you have selected. The changes can be tested first and your staff given tuition on the new order-processing software prior to "going live".

6.

SECURITY AND "SCAMS"

Security issues on the internet are becoming a veritable nightmare, and as the scams get more sophisticated, our enjoyment of surfing is jeopardised – and we all lose out! We have hackers (some good, some bad), krackers, spammers, viruses, Trojan horses, cookies, spyware, and all the anti-this-stuff software and firewalls crawling all over your computer and the ba****ds seem to contrive to screw-up your machine just when you need it most! Do you sense a smidgin of frustration in there somewhere? But I'm sure that if you've done any amount of internet surfing you'll know exactly what I mean.

We Are All Targets Now

It didn't used to be like that, ah the good old days! However, as the internet has burgeoned into the sophisticated multi-media dimensions of the present we have had to suffer an ever-increasing threat of intrusion into our machines and our lives. The security measures available now are much better at providing a stable platform whilst we are on-line, but we have to be much better informed about just how these systems are protecting us and what to do if they don't. Backing-up crucial on-line systems, ensuring firewalls are secure, and anti-virus, anti-spyware, anti-spamware are in place, are all critically necessary these days, and that's just for browsing the internet! If you run your browser on a PC with a Microsoft operating system and a Microsoft Explorer browser then you are more likely to suffer security problems, simply because it is the most popular system in the world and hence becomes, de-facto, a target for hackers and scammers. Although many will say that Microsoft asked for it because they left not just the back door (to the operating system) open, but the whole back wall was missing! This was aptly proven on the win95/98 operating systems when a group of hackers wrote a Trojan horse called 'back office' which had to be clicked open from an email and duly installed itself on the unsuspecting users machine. The 'back office' didn't do anything bad – the hackers were simply showing Microsoft how exposed their operating system was. Not all hackers are quite so obliging of course and there are many ways, too complex to go into here, whereby they can take control of any aspect of your computer – without you knowing!

Hackers – Black or White?

Did you know that hackers and krackers often work in groups and have their own international conventions (don't believe me - try searching 'hacker conventions') – most will claim that they are only doing it in order to get into computer security employment (yeah – right)! Others are openly defiant anarchists – the sort that take someone's packaged software and supplies it free to everyone just because they can (it should be noted that this author has often used copied software – but only in the cause of education – which is legal, right!) – or bypassing the poor music publisher's royalties by copying music illegally over the internet. The internet has always had elements of this type of anarchy (i.e. copying stuff to others is just sharing – isn't it?) and particularly for clever programmers – and I tend to say why the hell not – but the stakes are getting higher all the time and it's everyone that suffers from having to have the extra levels of security.

Internet Regulation

In America there have been a number of organisations prosecuted for allowing (facilitating?) the copying of music files, and even some companies that provide software which allows peer to peer networking to be set up (easier for person to person copying) are being sued, even though they are not in charge of what is, or isn't, copied! The point being that national regulation of what is happening on the internet is ratcheting up the laws on what is/isn't acceptable on the internet. All ISP's in Britain, for instance, now have to have a little "black box"(try searching for the 'RIP Act UK' - The Regulation of Investigatory Powers Act) on their servers to allow access by government security services (well it is long after 1984 after all!).

The Dreaded Spam E-mail

The one group of people that I really can't abide, however, is "spammers" – those creepy "entrepreneurs" who claim to be in "marketing". It is alleged that approximately 80% of all emails are spam (i.e. unsolicited emails) and it remains one of the webs biggest problems, for both individuals and companies. America has recently implemented the CAN-SPAM Act, but it has not provided the panacea that was intended, and has only reduced unlawful spam by a few percentage points. Microsoft have been slightly more successful with the alleged "king of spam", one Scott Richter, who was recently fined $7m – he is said to be responsible for 38 billion emails per year! Another notorious pair of spammers, Jessica DeGroot and Jeremy James (they were high on the spam watchdog's website "Spamhaus"), alleged to have made $24m from their enterprise, where they sent bulk emails containing false email addresses, only got fined $7,500, <u>although,</u> they did get a 9 year jail sentence!

Which brings me to the biggest security hole in most people's computers – emails. Now, emails, as we know, are a wonderful means of communication – which is why the scammers love them – why, well you are often the one who invites these emails into your computer, and this is when your guard is down – you think you have got all your protection in place – the firewall (no good – you've invited the email in), the anti-spam (your software can't check everything – especially if it's an unknown virus or Trojan horse), you think the email address is "kosha" (it's easy for a programmer to falsify the email address of the sender), and you hit that interesting link in the email ('cos you're curious), and shazam – you've just taken the bait.

Spam and Scam

This scam is called "phishing" and relies on the email recipient taking the bait (i.e. clicking on a link within an email message) – it must be said that most spammers are legally correct and allow you to instantly cancel and do you no harm - they come under the alternative title of "speculative marketing" (whatever!). These may be merely pointing out the advantages of their product/website and guiding you to look further into this. However, some are not quite what they seem – and this is where many scams are perpetrated. It may be they want your bank account number and password (they may give you a link to your on-line bank and present you with an identical screen to your bank's BUT once you have keyed in your account number and password they've got you – bye, bye money).

They may want you to accept a "too good to be true" offer - traditional spam would target the areas of:- lottery winner (or the Nigerian Prince who wants to deposit money in your bank account scam – yeah people are still falling for this old chestnut!), mortgages / loans (just give us your bank details and we will laugh all the way to ....), medication – (viagra anyone? – or the sick ones with cures for the incurable), and pornography – (mugs away – these guys are the masters of scamming; they invented it!) – or they may want to persuade you to buy certain stock (the latest scam is targeting stocks and shares) they massage you and others with a mixture of real stories and marketing lies about a targeted stock and then suddenly stop – everyone gets worried and sells – the stock-price goes down below market value quickly and they mop it up and make a huge profit!

The Scams are Getting Bigger

You think I'm kidding – the scams are getting very sophisticated – a recent admission from the Times On-Line (June 16th 2005 "Beware: You have mail" by Steven Downes, their On-Line Business Editor) apologises if you've recently received an email from "our business@timesonline.co.uk and they hope "that you won't have opened it, or any attachment therein" (only slightly embarrassed, then!). They further warned of "dire warnings from NISCC", the UK Government's National Infrastructure Security Co-ordination Centre, about the "biggest co-ordinated attack the world has seen since Operation Desert Storm." (the NISCC - who dey eh! Check them out and see what you think - I think they mean MI5's Cheltenham HQ, but then I am prone to paranoia!). It is not only the massive scale of the attack that has taken this scam to another level, but also the sophistication

– they've used social engineering research to ensure that recipients take the bait! Most of the emails are targeted at government departments and corporate businesses – however all of us will suffer in some way if the level of these attacks keeps rising. Perhaps more worrying is the fact that institutions, such as the CBI, are jumping up and down demanding something must be done (always a worrying sign), meaning of course that the government should be doing it (i.e. curbing our freedom of rights – normally!)

Don't Bug Me

It is always possible to track where most people are when on-line through their IP address (Internet Protocol address which identifies exactly where the computer is in the world) – however there are websites that hide this information and effectively allow anonymous surfing. This can be for malicious intent or more likely, these days, people are using them to simply avoid getting all the spam emails clogging up their mailboxes (e.g. www.bugmenot.com). It seems to be more and more common for websites that are offering some freebie, or service, are forcing you into compulsory registration of your details, which will always insist on an email address – and they are also checking that the email address exists before you have completed the form or only give you the access password via email, thus forcing you to give your email address. You are then bugged every five minutes with further spam – OK you can usually send an email to cancel, but it becomes an onerous task after a while.

Hijacking Your Phone Line

Another favourite scam, although now made more difficult by the telecom providers, is where the user dials onto the internet and is re-directed onto making a high-priced phone-link to a different provider (who could be anywhere in the world). This scam has mainly been stopped now but I bring it up just to highlight what "cookies" can do. A cookie is what can be deposited on your computer just by visiting a website – most are simply there to provide an enhancement to the website experience (e.g. a cookie might keep track of your interests on their site and show you latest updates of that thing), however, cookies are capable of being used in a malicious way.

Cookies are programs, and the scam previously mentioned would drop your phone-line to your usual ISP, then dial an expensive line of their own, and allow you to continue surfing at an extortionate rate – you only find out when you get your rather large telephone bill! Cookies can be disallowed from most browsers now, but this can mean that you miss out on some functionality of the web site or that your browser could behave strangely on some websites where cookies are used. Again, most websites have an ethical viewpoint on the use of cookies – unfortunately they are used, more and more, unethically by hackers and this spoils everyone's surfing experience.

Blocking Cookies

Cookies started out as simply an addition to web-programmers that allowed them to collect marketing information about a surfer's likes and dislikes. Typically they would sit on a users computer and collect information about what the surfer was doing, what information they were looking for, what they were buying, etc. I have always been wary of this type of intrusion – they are spying on you from your own computer, for gods sake! Hence the proliferation of spyware software in recent years – this type of software is manly dealing with the liability of cookies on your liberty. The good news is that most browsers now have strict guidelines for what they will allow cookies to do, and more importantly what they cannot do. Many of the loopholes that used to allow these programs to take control of your computer have been severely curtailed. The bad news is that more well informed hackers are coming on-stream all the time and they use more and more sophistication to get through the security.

Counter Measures

Against this scenario of attack whilst surfing there are a number of counter-measures:- anti-spyware software, website authorisation (such as Verisign, www.verisign.com – websites can take-up authorisation with certain bodies that undertake to check sites for content and ethical behaviour), firewalls, proxy-servers, and routers.

The sophistication of the hackers where 'cookies' or 'spyware' is concerned has caused a revolution in the way that browsers and anti-virus software companies have responded. This and other security risks associated with the internet has caused a major change in the way that businesses have approached the biggest security challenge of the twenty-first century. By far the safest option with web-access is to only allow access through a router and/or a proxy server; whereby your company networked computers are divorced from damage by being remote from the most obvious internet dangers. Small companies cannot afford to allow their operators direct access to the web, it is rapidly becoming too dangerous to do this. Emails should also be answered only by a dedicated computer (think of it as your own email post-office), which is outside your LAN (local area network) and outside your firewalls, routers, etc. Only once emails have been virus-checked and scrutinised for authenticity should they be allowed inside your office network firewalls.

The Importance of Controlling Spam

Your email should be set-up to siphon-off spam (unsolicited) emails into its own directory, so that it can be dealt with separately. Email settings should also disallow HTML (emails that look like web-pages) and images – viruses and Trojan horses can be hidden in these. If these basic precautions are adhered to then, barring operator error, this will keep 99% of problems getting anywhere near your LAN-based system. I cannot reiterate too much the vital importance of efficient backup routines and that operator error will cause you more problems than the hackers – the more complex the attack from the hackers, the more complex the means of combating these attacks – your staff will need continual bouts of education in order to play 'catch-up'.

Website Security

Until now we have only considered the major areas of attack through internet browsers and email – however, your website is also under attack! Many ISP's have, in recent years, been forced to defend their own systems and servers from ever-increasing attacks on their security. In general ISP security has been good – but they are coming under a concerted barrage of attacks, not only from hackers but also from governments and other bodies regarding everything from scams to ethics to definitions of everything in-between.

OK, I know it's difficult to understand just what sort of thing is happening with ISP's and websites, so I'm going to try and give you a number of examples to illustrate the kind of problems occurring here:

Website Attacks

Recently, I logged on to a client's website in order to make some updates and was shocked to discover that the 'permissions' on the main 'directories' were all wrong – the website had obviously been under attack! One of the main security arrangements on a website are the directory and file 'permissions' that allow access restrictions to browsers – most websites only allow access to one directory and only allow those browsers to read information and execute certain programs to provide the required interactive communications – none normally allow the ability of browsers to change or 'write' files (i.e. change your website pages or information without your knowledge) – yet this is the state that I found my client's website – anything could be changed (from anywhere in the world remember) – and the ISP was, at first, denying that this could happen – although they later, reluctantly, agreed that this is exactly what <u>had</u> happened!!!

My response was to assume that security of my client's website had been compromised and immediately re-installed the website from backup sources – any of the files on the ISP's servers could have been changed – it seemed that some of my files had been made capable of change (i.e., made write-enabled) so I could only assume that these may have contained a virus or a Trojan-horse – by going to a backup situation this prospect was contained.

Attack or Incompetence?

It wasn't long ago that a major bank was compromised when it was discovered that their website was allowing access to customer account information from a file on their main website primary directory. This was obviously the result of a mistake on the part of the programmer – most programmers using web-languages would hide their confidential files at a deeper directory level than the primary directory, and they certainly wouldn't allow them to be read – this was the result of using an amateur, or inexperienced, programmer! However, this underlines the problems that are inherent in the burgeoning web programming arena – a general business failure to understand the basic concepts and essentials of internet security. Many businesses expect the programmer to understand the whole of their business, and also to accept the cheapest quote for their work – for work that is highly central to their commercial success, or failure.

The Automated Email

Another typical example recently occurred where an on-line bank sent automated emails (spam???) to its customers with other peoples account details on them!!! They were so embarrassed that they gave all those concerned a compensatory payment – as well as having to give everyone new account numbers, change all those standing orders, direct debits, etc. etc. (would have loved to have been a fly on the marketing departments wall when it was discovered what they'd done!).

The whole point is that there are hackers out there who are continually trawling websites for information, continually probing for weaknesses – and finding them! Nine times out of ten the businesses that get caught out by hackers will never admit to it - it is one thing to have your security compromised – it is another to suffer the shame and loss of business that would result from media headlines.

There are also many programmers out there who although they may be capable of supplying services and facilities on your website, they do not know enough about the essential security considerations required from a medium which is under constant attack from more and more sophisticated hackers. Most of these attacks can be rebuffed by the vigilance and security barriers of the ISP – but if your web programmer leaves your web files open to scrutiny then the ISP can do little about this.

It's Complicated!

Many programming languages used on web sites can easily be seen by hackers and if the web programmer has omitted essential checks they can be altered and used as a means of getting at the data being filed on that website. Furthermore many of these programs have originated on other utility websites that offer the use of their programs under licence, or are in the open source or freeware arena. These programs may have security risks associated with them and there are, of course, disreputable sites that will promote 'free' programs in order to exploit them at a later date when they have become central to your website data gathering process! Most people can do little about this type of hacking and are at the mercy of their web designer's ability to write secure and impregnable systems. However, many ISP's are working hard to keep hackers at bay and they often employ their own extra security – particularly where email is concerned – they know that their own systems are vulnerable to attack if they don't.

Web security will always be a problem – for every programmer coming up with a more secure way of doing things there will be a hacker capable of getting round it. This is, of course, a natural evolution of events and will always be thus – however it is as well to consider the risks, attempt to foresee most eventualities, and have preparations ready for the worst scenario. Your first line of defence is a well-educated and vigilant workforce.

7.

SEARCH-ENGINE SUBMISSIONS AND OPTIMISATION

Type 'search-engine optimisation' (or 'SEO') into a search-engine like Google and you'll get a plethora of companies telling you much the same thing – that <u>they</u> are the best, and that they can get your website into the top 10 search-results on Google, Yahoo and MSNsearch. Whether they <u>can</u> achieve this ethically is subject to a high degree of scepticism from this author, and may well depend on the amount of money you are prepared to spend!

DIY Optimisation

Much of what they can do for your site is straightforward and can be achieved easily with a little bit of hard work. Search-engine optimisation is about getting the best search results for your website for particular word-searches, and this will always be a changing feast – clearly not everyone can be first and your ranking will change as the search-engines change the rules – which they do all the time. If you start out by doing your own 'optimisation' and marketing then you will understand what works for you – you will be in control and will realise that by continually updating your site you will establish a positive website presence within a linked community of associated sites.

As the search-engines change the rules (to try to gain an advantage over rivals) then rankings will change and the way in which your site is optimised will need to change. For example, at one time optimisers would set-up 'doorway pages' (or cloaking pages) which were pages that had lots of repetition of keywords (keyword spamming) but would make little sense to surfers – then when you clicked on these you would be redirected (this is simply done) to the <u>actual</u> home page of the site – this allowed extra advantage as you could set up a doorway page for each search-engine and optimise the page for that engine. Doing this now runs the risk of getting you banned from the search-engines.

Links Show Popularity – Don't They?

In recent years Google placed greater emphasis on the number of links that a website had (both inbound and outbound links – i.e. links to others and links from others) and the other search-engines followed suit. This led to a huge increase in link-farming – the optimisers started to create their own groups of inter-related linking sites – these sites did little else than create the impression that a site had lots of links and therefore rankings were artificially increased!

Guessing the Search-Engine's Methods

However, Google responded by finding the link-farms and demoted any websites that were using them – and now link-farming is a big 'No No' and again might even get your site banned from Google altogether. Optimisation is the process of your site trying to gain advantage – but clearly the optimisation process – although it has some basic rules – is always going to be trying to second-guess what the search-engines are doing – it becomes more of an art than a science, and some would say that it's more 'smoke and mirrors'. Although they wouldn't let it be known I believe that many

SEO's are still using risky practices to promote websites – when (not if) they are found out you may find your website rapidly demoted – but by then the SEO will have banked their fee!

The search-engine marketing industry is a maturing phenomena – one simply has to look at the rising share price of Google to realise the advantages of being in the race. The big three – Google, Yahoo, and MSNsearch all vie for our interest when we search in order to distract us into clicking the sponsored (paid-for) links, which is their bread and butter.

We Don't Like Ads!

A previous method used was the use of banner advertising and the 'pay per click' means of advertising, which was taken-up big-time by the corporate websites. Many surfers have spent most of their time avoiding these along with the iniquitous pop-up windows that won't go away and prevent you using your browsers back button. So the search-engines used other things to attract us – we get the contextual ads like Google's 'adword' and Yahoo's 'Overture', which at least giving you added benefit in that they follow the basic search-words that you searched on (i.e. if you searched for 'lawn-care' you might get a contextual ad for lawn-mowers, fertilisers, etc.).

Then each search-engine was doing its own add-on 'toolbar' for your browser, professing to give you extra search capability, but at the same time spying on what your surfing patterns are! An increasing number of my friends are seriously worried (pissed off?) that this intrusive behaviour is being used by search-engines, and are either refusing to use them or shifting from Microsoft's Internet Explorer to browsers such as Firefox (www.mozilla.org/products/firefox/) and Opera (www.opera.com) – (a) because they don't like being spied on and (b) because they get less hassle with viruses and cookies with Trojan-horses (most are associated with internet explorer simply because it's the most common browser).

Search-Engines Rule OK

Then came the extra categories of searching – searching for music, videos, books, etc. and so it continues – each of the major search engines has to extend the search process and provide the best search results possible – we hope! When we try to understand the way in which each search-engine ranks its search results it becomes a highly complex process – and I would suggest that the optimisation process is in danger of becoming redundant, purely because of the level of sophistication of the search-engines.

It is certainly easier for the search-engine optimisers to say what you shouldn't do, than what you should do, to achieve higher rankings! A note here about Page-Rank – this is a common ranking system used by the search-engines to 'classify' a website. Although each engine will use different means to calculate this figure it is regarded as a means of defining a site's 'popularity' – if you download Google's toolbar (toolbar.google.com/en_GB/) it contains a PR visual telling you what the PR is for the site you are looking at. Page-Rank is a number between 0 and 10 – the higher the number the better your ranking.

So, what shouldn't you do? What might get your site banned from the search-engines?

What Might Get Your Site Banned?

❑ Doorway Pages or cloaking – as already mentioned
❑ Submitting multiple URL's for the same site – e.g. submitting www.yoursite.com and www.yoursite.com/index.html
❑ Hidden text - an old method of spamming with keywords that the surfer can't see because the text is the same colour as the background colour.
❑ Spamming – cramming your pages with repetitions of keywords purely to up your keyword prominence.
❑ Link-farming – already mentioned above
❑ Multiple identical sites – some optimisers will set-up virtually identical sites on different domains but interlinked to increase linking – the sites have the same content.
❑ Excessive page–linking – Google will object to more than 100 links on any one page and downgrade your ranking accordingly

All of the above have been used in the past by search-engine optimisers to get better search-results, but now these methods are penalised – are you starting to get the picture – optimisers use the latest 'tricks' to boost their rankings and search-results, the search-engines then 'ban' or penalise the 'tricks' in an attempt to level the playing field.

Content Is King

The one thing that will never get penalised and will always remain top of the agenda when search-engines analyse your site is good content (copy) – it is, after all, the essence of what they are trying to index. If you remember nothing else about optimisation – remember this – content is king, the better your content and the judicial use of keywords and key phrases within that content is your primary goal in getting good search-engine positioning. The next major criteria is good inbound links from associates (or affiliates) that have good page-ranking themselves of 5 or above.

No More Automated Submissions?

When you submit your site to search-engines you are simply telling them that you exist and that you want to be indexed in their databases around the world. It used to be possible to do this automatically, and there are sites who will do this for you, or more correctly, there used to be – recently (earlier this year) I noticed that many of the websites offering submissions (just search on 'free website submissions') used to submit to most of the search-engines automatically – you would enter your website URL and off they would go.

However, this now seems to be the exception rather than the rule and most of these submission sites do no more than point you at the search-engine 'add-URL' page of each search-engine and you have to manually enter your details. This is obviously in response to a burgeoning number of submissions and the over-use of software such as Web-Position Gold, whose methods in the past fall mainly within the DON'T list above, and are largely redundant these days. Don't be fooled by the use of this type of 'submissions' software – their methods are far too outdated to be of much use and they are definitely disliked by the search-engines themselves (as lots of automated process impinge adversely on their systems).

The search-engine optimisers want you to think that the whole process of submissions and optimisation is a complex business that only <u>they</u> can understand – however, the number of tricks that they use will inevitably result in a downgrading by the search-engines at some point, and any temporary gain in positioning could easily be short-lived. Many are still using link-farming methods, in a variety of different guises, and the search-engine algorithms will discover this at some point – it is not a matter of 'if' but 'when'.

We Submit Your Site to 1000's of Search-Engines

Don't be fooled by the 'We submit to over 1000 search-engines' strategy either because this is not happening – yes, there are many small and insignificant (in the main) search-engines out there, but most of the search-engines use only a small number of basic directories and data-search engines. The main ones are:-

❑ Open Directory Project – a directory which is used by some of the major search-engines and is updated manually – submitting for inclusion is done manually and your site is checked for inclusion and may not be accepted if it doesn't fit the criteria – read the rules carefully (http://dmoz.org/add.html).

❑ Yahoo directory – Yahoo's own directory which you cannot enter manually – they have their own web-crawler (they used to use Google's – they are partnered to MSNSearch) which creates and maintains this database – although I believe you might be included if you pay the $299 required as a commercial site to be included by Yahoo themselves – should be unnecessary – but then money talks.

- ❏ Lycos – an established directory
- ❏ Some engines are pay-per-click search-engines only and in order to submit to these you must manually submit your details and open an account with your credit-card. At the time of writing these include GoTo, Overture, FindWhat, Kanoodle, Google-Adwords, GoClick and others
- ❏ Inktomi – Is a partnered search-engine database which doesn't accept manual submissions, but gets its information through the use of a web-crawler or from other 'partners' – e.g. submitting to MSN (http://beta.search.msn.com/docs/submit.aspx) will also get you indexed on partners Yahoo, AOL, Netscape, Iwon and others
- ❏ Teoma – Is a web-crawler search-engine database which doesn't accept manual submissions and powers Ask-Jeeves amongst others
- ❏ AllTheWeb – Another web-crawler search-engine database
- ❏ Google – has its own search-engine database which it maintains through its web-crawler called Googlebot – submitting to Google (http://www.google.com/addurl) will get you onto this index – (if you have links to your site from a site already listed by Google then the Googlebot will automatically find and index you)

The above list caters for over 90% of the search-engine facilities found on the web and although it may appear confusing at first, it is somewhat less than the oft-claimed 'We will submit your site to thousands of search-engines'. By focussing on Google, The Open Directory and MSNSearch or Yahoo you will be covering most of your bases for free submissions, and although it may take some time before your site gets indexed (due to the sheer volume of websites coming onto the web each day), the web-crawlers will eventually (about a month – sometimes longer) find and index your site.

Web-Crawlers, Spiders, Robots

There is a way where you can tell the web-crawlers how often you want to be updated thereafter and this depends how often you will be making changes to your web pages. If the following HTML code is added to your home page (or index page) you can control how often the web-crawlers will visit your site:

```
<META name="revisit-after" content="15 days">
<META name="robots" content="index,follow">
```

This is fairly self-explanatory and will cause any robots (web-crawlers, spiders, bots - whatever!) to revisit your site every 15 days and re-index it by following from your home-page the links to other pages. This, of course, assumes that you will be updating your web-pages at least on a fortnightly basis – otherwise there is no point! I would advise that if you do nothing else at least change your home page regularly – the web-crawlers love to see changes and will automatically re-index the site – conversely if they never see changes they could drop your site from their 'to do list'.

You can tell whether your site has been 'crawled' (visited) by a web-crawler by looking in your sites log files – your ISP will have information of how to look in your logs and most web-crawlers will leave information on when you were last visited.

What Most Affects Your Page Ranking?

Your sites page-rank (PR) gives some indication of how often the web-crawlers will normally visit your site and this indicator depends heavily on the number and quality of your inbound links – i.e. if you have established good inbound links from sites whose page-rank is 5 or more then your site is likely to be visited more often. If you have no inbound links then you will find it hard to increase your page-rank – the thinking behind

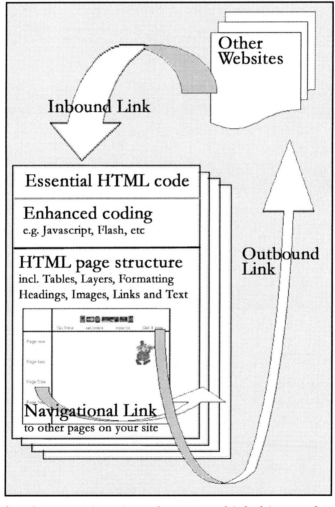

this is that busy, active sites that get a high hit rate because they are providing good dynamic, valuable content within a popular web neighbourhood are more likely to be updated more often.

Again we see how important content and linking becomes to search-engines and this should form the main thrust of improving your page-rank value and thus your site's popularity. Conversely, if your inbound links are coming from unpopular sites or from what the search-engine regards as a link-farm then this could adversely affect your page-rank to the point that a search-engine might drop your listing (link-farms are often considered as constituting a bad web neighbourhood) and some ISP's doing a lot of this type of 'spamming' can also get a bad reputation with search-engines.

Other major factors in improving your page-rank fall into three HTML categories: Essential HTML code, Enhanced coding, and HTML page structure, as in the diagram above.

Essential HTML Code and W3C

Essential HTML code comes at the start of your web-page and defines the essential elements of your page. The very first line determines the type of web document such as <!DOCTYPE HTML PUBLIC "-//W3C//DTD HTML 4.0 Transitional//EN"> and this should be a recognised label conforming to the World-Wide-Web-Consortium (W3C is at http://www.w3.org/) – if this is incorrect the web-crawlers may ignore you. If you go to the W3C website you can get your HTML code validated. A warning here about 'frame-based' sites – i.e. where your main navigation to your pages is in a 'frame' so that it stays the same (usually left of screen) whilst people surf through your pages in a separate frame (normally to the right of screen) – this was a popular way of constructing websites but is not part of the W3C future direction of HTML coding and, more importantly, is sometimes responsible for web-crawlers missing the main content of your web-pages.

The next most important 'tag' (HTML code type) is the title e.g. <title>Straightforward Publishing Self-Help Books – Home Page</title> which is a description of what your page is about. This should have essential keywords in it such that the search engines are capable of categorising it. The description tag is next as it is often used in search-listings as the description of your page. This tag (<meta name="description") used to be allied to a keywords tag (<meta name="keywords") which now tends to be ignored by the search-engines as they now prefer to find your keywords for themselves from your text content – this happened because of the tendency of optimisers to use 'spamming' (repetition of keywords). Your description should describe as precisely as possible what your site (or page) is about – it should contain your most important keywords and only be about 30 words long.

Enhanced Coding

Enhanced coding constitutes things such as Javascript, and Flash, which are things that your web-designer might use to add more interesting content or interactivity on the page. The essential message here is to try and avoid too much of this as it 'bloats' the coding – i.e. it is something the web-crawlers have to plough through before getting to anything that it deems important, which is the actual textual content. This sort of coding can often be externalised – put into an associated code file – and this helps a lot in maintaining good tidy code that the web-crawlers can easily follow.

The same is true of using CSS (Cascading Style Sheets) to do your text-formatting, in that it takes out a great deal of extraneous coding into an allied file and leaves the overall web-page a lot less cluttered with formatting code than it would otherwise be. All this will greatly improve the ratio of keywords to text, known as 'keyword density', and thus improve your overall Page-Ranking.

If your website designer intends to use enhanced techniques, such as Flash animations (don't use unless they are crucial to enhancing your main marketing direction), then be aware that any text or links used <u>within these</u> may not be picked up by the web-crawlers. Web-crawlers cannot get into these applications because of the programming constraints, although this may change. For instance, most web-crawlers are now capable of analysing 'pdf' files for text and links (these pdf files are a third-party means of allowing documents to be held and downloaded from websites and are considered worth indexing by search-engines because of the high level of 'content').

HTML Page Structure Coding

HTML page structure coding are the tags that control the structuring and formatting of the web-page 'body'. If you can imagine the web-crawler trying to create a structure of words in order to classify and index the most important words in your content, then obviously headings and sub-headings will be important and the <H1>, <H2>, etc headings tags will be vital in this process – try to make sure that they reflect your keyword importance in terms of where you want to be classified. For instance, on the Straightforward Publishing website it is important to re-iterate that the site is about books and publishing, it is also part of the ethos of the site that they are about self-help publishing and therefore the headings reflect this by using sub-headings with these keywords in order to re-enforce these.

The content is then scanned by the web-crawlers who will be attempting to find associated or similar words and then indexing the site under these main headings and relative (contextual) links using keywords and keyword phrases. Getting the right mix between using a good smattering of keywords amongst unique and interesting content is difficult, but it is worth playing with the mix to improve your Page-Ranking. The search-engines will then index the site under 'books' and 'publishing' and 'self-help books', etc.

Regular Changes = Additional Indexing

The Straightforward Publishing website will then be competing within these classifications as to who has the best page-ranking. These classifications can be affected by changes to the wording in all the above-mentioned tags and in the content – if it was decided that it would be beneficial to try attracting more writers, then by changing the home page to include keywords or phrases such as 'new writers wanted', 'budding authors', 'writing a book', etc. will get the site classified in slightly different, and additional, indexing areas pointing to the site. By adding a page outlining how these new authors would contact the company this gives extra keywords and content for the web-crawlers to include (it is best to keep additional pages short and concise so that they form a complete topic). Your indexing can increase according to the page changes that you include – an active, dynamic site is more likely to gain Page-Ranking through this means.

Other important areas are: images – these should have a description of the image (in the 'alt' area), which includes keywords where possible, and links – these again should, in the text area, contain keywords describing what the link is about. The use of other HTML attributes like tables, layers, hidden text, etc. can give the web-crawlers difficulties if the coding is too complicated – anything which detracts from your text content will run the risk of causing the web-crawler to give-up and look at the next site on its list. Good clean code and clear interesting content with secondary page links that re-iterate the content of your home page headings and sub-headings is what the crawlers are looking for.

Although the above may seem over-simplified, especially when the optimisers are keen to make it look complicated – however, don't get sucked into the trap of the optimiser's rhetoric - you can do much of the work yourself as regards marketing your website and improving your website's ranking. Make sure that your web-designer keeps to the above basic recipe of producing good clean coding, and make sure that your copy is unique, contains the keywords appropriate to your business, and is updated carefully on a regular basis.

8.

MARKETING

Marketing is vital if you want your website to become successful – if you think that just creating a website, no matter how wonderful it might be, you can sit back and wait for the world to surf in – you will be waiting a long time! Even though you may have submitted your site to all the search-engines your site will be a long way down the search-results – if it appears at all. When you are starting out the search-engines will not give you a very high ranking until you have completed some very necessary marketing exercises. The first task is to raise your search-engine page-ranking.

Raising Your Page-Ranking

The most important way of raising your PR is by setting-up reciprocal links - this is what many SEO's would do to raise your site's profile. In order to do this use Google and/or Yahoo to do searches on your keywords, or phrases, and work through the list of websites that are allied to, but not direct competitors to, your business <u>and</u> that already have a good rage-rank of 5 or more (linking to sites with lower PR will not lift your site). Check their site to see if they have a links page, and if so, send a friendly email to the webmaster of the site (best to find out a name or email address) giving them your website address, a bit of information as to what your website is, and does, and suggest a good URL link that you would be prepared to put on your site's 'associates' (or links) page.

Your home page should have a link to your links page – normally placed at the bottom of the home page so that if they are not interested in your site's products or services they can surf directly to any useful links from your site. On the web the term 'affiliates' is often used instead, although I consider this term to be more formal, in a cold commercial marketing sense, in that marketing companies have built-up whole massed ranks of 'affiliates' for major pay-per-click campaigns - try searching on 'UK affiliates' and you'll see what I mean.

Make Some Friends!

Your links page is important to your site's ranking and should be titled something like 'associates' or 'associated partners' - don't just give a list of links but describe some of the essentials of what each linked website is about and how it is a favoured partner of your business. Group your links according to their perceived categories and treat the marketing of your linked associates seriously – review them regularly and try contacting them for mutual marketing campaigns.

If you aim to achieve at least 50 good reciprocal links to sites, then your page-rank will be significantly increased. It is of interest that at the moment Google has a limit on its web-crawler that no page is 'crawled' further than 100 links – now, most web-pages, forgive me if I'm wrong, are unlikely to have 100 links unless it's a link-farm, or, dare I say it, an SEO affiliated site! Google is trying to throttle the link-farms – you heard it here first folks – but link-farming is here to stay, even if the SEO's call it something else and have to work a little harder to disguise them! If your link-marketing is based more on friendly correspondence (as I have described), than commercial placement, then your link-marketing will be considerably more productive.

Advertorials and Product Placement

It is worth looking out for better opportunities on certain sites during the above exercise – look for sites that are OK with placing links within the body of its pages – you may be expected to pay for these, as a direct advertising effort, but try the 'you scratch my back' approach first! This approach works in much the same way as 'infomercials' or product placement in the film industry, or 'advertorials' in magazines or newspapers. This product-placement linking from within a web-page's content is more likely to generate traffic – links pages are seldom visited by surfers – the main reason for having them is to raise your PR and your positioning in the search-engine results. You can pay for adverts on some of the more popular sites, a site with a PR of 7 would be receiving millions of hits per day, your advert on a site such as this, especially if it offers something free, will bring a lot of traffic to your site.

Be Perceived as an Expert

Your marketing efforts are more likely to be rewarded if you make positive attempts to carve a reputation, within your web neighbourhood, of professionalism and commitment. When you establish reciprocal links, your linking partner will want to scrutinise your site, they should perceive your site to be professional and comprehensive – they will want reassurance that your link to them puts them in a good light. If they see your site as a strong marketing force within your mutual web neighbourhood then they will happily provide reciprocal linking. There is no problem in you setting up your link to them first, such that when they look at your site they already see their site being promoted – if they don't respond or don't want to link back then you simply take the link off.

The Newsletter

Once you start to build your reciprocal links you can think of further contact with your associates to build a regular forum of mutual marketing. A common way to do this is through production of a regular newsletter about your website, your company products and services, which would contain interesting articles and information useful to both customers and associates. This newsletter should contain advertising of your associates' websites, which provides a marketing 'hook' for prospective associates – free advertising.

Your newsletter can be provided as a hook for customers via email on your website – they would sign-up for regular email delivery as long as it is perceived as having value – be sure to always allow people to opt-out of your email list, and don't send too much marketing hype. The occasional interesting mail is fun, too much is annoying – it is important not to upset your visitors. For example, if we take the previous analogy of a website selling lawn-mowers, then we might commission articles on how the Lords' cricket pitch is kept in shape during test matches from the head-groundsman, alongside technical articles on different types of lawn-repair techniques. The point is, it doesn't have to be just about lawn-mowers - by creating a more general appeal your company is perceived as being an 'expert' in the field – your associates, who might be in the grass seed or turf-supply business, would be pleased that they are your link-partner and that they have free advertising in your fascinating newsletter.

Incentive Marketing

In marketing, incentives generally work – for instance, if you offer your link-associate's staff a special discount on your popular products or services in exchange for promoting your site, then you would be on your way to creating a dynamic marketing environment within your web-neighbourhood. You must look carefully at the products and services that you are selling, within the context of your web competitors, in order to establish your own unique selling points. Remember, unlike ordinary shopping, the next shop is just a click away, and there are likely to be a number of sites selling similar things – what is so special about your site – what will make customers come to you?

It's not all about discounting or being cheaper than the next guy – although this might help – setting-up loss-leaders to incentivise people, or creating a group of products (bundled) at a very cheap price are all common methods. For example, using the lawn-mower analogy again, you might do a deal with some of your associates to offer, with a discounted mower, a free bag of lawn-repair, a free pair of lawn-edging shears, and a booklet about 'Looking after your lawn' (preferably with a famous gardener's endorsement) – you could contact your associates to place your advert for this offer and your associates would, in turn, be advertised in your booklet. There are many ways to incentivise your link-associates, look for the unique selling points that you can offer and above all – use your imagination!

Organic Growth and Web 'Real Estate'

OK so here's the real secret – the internet thrives on organic (i.e. natural) growth – the SEO's have been chasing this fact ever since the internet was invented - and your marketing has to grow organically, right across your web neighbourhood, if your site is to be successful. Regular surfers, in the main, try to ignore all attempts at being diverted from their objective – when searching for something specific we'll either find it, or something close, in our first 2 or 3 searches. As surfers we will rarely go deeper than the first page of our search-results, but we may, just, be attracted by clever placement of contextual links. This is why the contextual advertising of Overture and Google's Adwords work so well – they give additional value to the 'organic' search and become part of the information collecting process when shopping.

It is known that young surfers are less likely to click on sponsored links than the older surfer, and the tendency, when shopping on-line, is for surfers to research, very carefully, the offers and details of what they want to buy. The SEO's and advertisers know this, and don't just rely on one method - instead they try to spread their adverts and advertorials (and articles and ezines, and pay per click, and ....) across as much internet 'real estate' as possible.

Ezines, Classified Ads and Groups

The SEO's are in the business of creating this web-presence for any site, they use all the tricks of the trade – advertorials (product-placement), Ezines (if you write articles for these you can get a link for free), paid placement (try the 'you scratch my back.... approach), classified ads (use every opportunity as long as it is not harming you), group discussion and forums (groups.google.com or groups.yahoo.com), etc. You can do all this too – it's not difficult once you've got going – and you stay in control of your own marketing thrust.

More 'real estate'

Ezines are a useful arena for your advertising – If you find an Ezine (or Webzine) which covers or touches on your business, then by advertising (rates are generally low) with them you are immediately getting to a wide readership that is directly interested in your web neighbourhood (try searching on 'UK ezine marketing'). A useful tip here is to offer a freebie to attract people to your site – for example, again using our lawn-mower analogy, we could provide a downloadable pdf file called "How to choose a lawn-mower", which would contain useful information from your experts covering: different types of mower, handy tips on grass care, useful accessories, price guide, etc. Your advert then simply points people to your website where they can download this for free (you might want to ask for an email address for follow-up marketing).

The beauty of this type of approach is that not only are the customers drawn in to your site, they are the one's who are currently thinking of buying your products and a follow-up could be turned into a sale.

Articles, especially if they provide high-quality information, are invaluable and are <u>known</u> to generate high web-traffic. If they are strategically placed on popular sites they will enhance your hit-rate, as long as they are perceived as useful, interesting and informative – if you have staff interested in technical specifications of your products, or with specific knowledge or experience in their trade, then make use of their expertise by getting them to write a number of regular contributions to your marketing efforts.

Pay Per Click

Pay Per Click (PPC and its variations – Cost Per Click, etc) advertising is useful and should be instigated on some of the keywords (and keyword phrases) of your business. You are vying with others for these keywords, and only paying for the click-through, so think about your choice and try changing the keywords to see what works best for your business. Essentially you are buying into paid-for ('contextual' is best) advertising with your own keywords and can define how these will be used, as well as controlling how much you want to pay per month (check out Google Adwords at https://adwords.google.com/select/). The big advantage of this type of advertising is that it will normally appear on the first page of the search-results for that search-engine's searches.

Banner Exchanges

Banner Ads can be exchanged and there are some excellent banner exchange sites on the web. Search carefully for the larger ones who give good ratings and allow you a range of sites that would enhance your web neighbourhood.

Once Your Web Traffic Increases

Once your web-traffic has been increased and become profitable you can look at the various revenue streams to generate extra profit. For instance, use Google's Adsense to generate contextual adverts on your own site. These are similar to the old banner ads but you only get contextual ads (in text and applied to the content on your page) so you are still within an 'organic' environment. Although these contextual adverts might be taking traffic away from your site, they give you some revenue, which helps to offset the cost of your own advertising budget. Other revenue can come from selling advertising in your regular newsletter, selling banner ads, product placements, etc., plus commissions can be earned from your associate's links (for each time the link is used to go to the associate).

Signing up for discussion groups in your area of business can also be a useful means of generating more perceived 'expertise' – these should not be used cynically to just advertise your site, but if you are seen as a useful and <u>contributing</u> group member then your reputation will be your advert.

The Blogger

You might set-up your own discussion group, or blogger site, in the current parlance, for it's much the same thing. A blog site is simply a website that allows discussion on whatever the blog site is about – it started as a diary log of someone's life – the famous Baghdad Blogger wrote about what was happening in Baghdad – it's now difficult to actually find his site, try searching Google and you'll find so many other sites latching onto his title.

Blogging has become popular as a means of finding out what is actually going on in any area of modern life – some have remarked that every blogger thinks they are a journalist – and there is some truth in this. However, it has generated a whole following on the web and where there is a market there is prime 'real estate' for your marketing.   Just by taking part in a blogger's discussions you can leave a link to your own site - if it has some relevance – even if it's just your email address from your domain, you are creating inbound links, which may be indexed by the web-crawlers, especially if it's a popular blog with a high page-ranking.

Why set up a blog site – well, it's the newest buzz on the web and it's not really seen as corporate or commercial. Furthermore, there are more than 40 million sites worldwide and it's all about interaction – it's seen as a connection between people who are talking specifically around a particular subject. The marketing is, therefore, from person to person and recommendations are considered more 'real' or valuable. Traditional marketing methods are getting more expensive and returning less – blog sites provide a new and immediate feedback – users ask others on the blog-site direct questions about where to get the best deals on the web – it is the old 'word of mouth' scenario – and web-marketing companies are rather nervous about this direction – again the surfer is dodging the ads! Corporate companies are beginning to get in on the act (surprise, surprise!) and the value of the blog site is being eroded because of this – however, at the moment you should consider getting into this rich seam of web 'real estate' – but make sure you create a good one – it does need working at, but they are cheap and accessible to set up (try searching on 'blogger website templates', or 'The Big Blog Co').

In Conclusion

In conclusion, marketing is what will bring your 'shop' into the 'high street' of the internet – without it your website will never be successful. Be sure that you are providing unique selling points within your web neighbourhood and keep a sharp eye on your competitors – web-surfers are very fickle, if they see a good deal elsewhere they'll be off like a flock of migrating birds. Keep track of the latest trends in web-marketing – do this by checking the marketing guru's (search on 'UK marketing' – American marketing can be very much geared to the home country). One guru to take a look at is Harvey Segal (just search on his name – this is NOT an endorsement), who does give some useful tips – however, it must be remembered that this guy makes his money from the likes of you, so be warned you may finding yourself signing up for all sorts of things, try to resist, and adapt his ideas to your own situation. Finally, let me wish you good luck with your enterprise – be persistent and your site will be successful.

.NET	A Microsoft networking environment used in web interaction of databases, etc.
Advertorials	Adverts masquerading as editorial or instructive copy.
ASP	Active Server Pages – Microsoft scripting language delivering 'on the fly' web pages.
ASP.NET	Microsoft network support for active server pages (ASP).
Associates, Associated businesses	Your marketing 'friends' – suppliers, other businesses that you work closely with.
Banner ads	Image-based website adverts linking to the site that places the advert.
Blogger or blog site	A blogger is simply someone who sets up a website to put a diary-style regular commentary up on the web – these can often maintain a discussion or forum style of interactivity.
Capture of funds	The act of debiting funds from a credit card at the card-owners bank of origin.
cloaking	The act of deceiving search-engines by using false home pages and using re-directed URL's to go to the real home page.

content or copy	The actual text used in your web page which is searched by search-engines and used to index your site through a combination of your keywords
contextual	In the same context – the way search-engines index your keywords or key-phrases as synonyms, etc
cookie	A program which launches itself when you access it's web-page – they sit in your computer and generally provide additional interactive 'value'. Often they provide the source company with marketing information or, if bad, do untold damage to your computer system!
CSS	Cascading Style Sheets – a way of allocating text styles to your web pages and producing better HTML code.
domain	The named space given to you by your Internet Service Provider
domain name	The name of your website on the world wide web (e.g. www.yourname.com)
doorway pages	Associated with 'cloaking' in that these are the pages that are used to enhance your page-rank for each search-engine – they are never accessed as they contain re-directs to the actual home page.

downloads	You can 'download' information from websites – try right-clicking on your mouse and using 'Save As' – all types of media can be downloaded off the web.
e-commerce	Electronic transfer of funds for goods via the internet.
e-mail	Electronic transfer of mail via the internet.
FAQ	Frequently Asked Questions – most websites have a page dedicated to this – they try to pre-empt the visitor's questions on the site.
firewall	This is operating system software protection on your computer that tries to protect you from other users of the internet and from computer virus attack.
Flash	This is a comprehensive and popular means of providing animation on computer pages.

Frame-based site	A website that uses 'frames' i.e. the screen is divided into different web-pages – one doing the navigation (left of screen) and one showing the actual page(right of screen). They are not regarded by the W3C as standard and web-crawlers can find them difficult to crawl.
Hacker, cracker, kraker, (whatever!)	Someone who uses programming and code-breaking for influence. There are good and bad hackers – some ply their trade just because they can!
Hidden text	Text can be hidden within a web-page by a number of means – one is making the colour of the text the same as the background – in the old days (yawn – I know!) this was used by SEO's to spam (keyword repetition) in order to gain search-engine positioning.
Hit rate	How many visitors you get to your site.
Home page	Your opening page to your site – this is often named 'index.html'
HTML	Hypertext Mark-Up Language – the coding of web-pages.
Inbound Links	Other websites linking to your site

ISP	Internet Service Provider – anyone who provides a service for the world wide web.
Javascript	A scripting language that is used in conjunction with HTML pages to provide greater interactivity.
jpeg	A type of image formatting used heavily on the web to show photographic images.
keyword	A word which is crucial to your business – are you a 'second-hand car salesman' then these are your keywords!!! It is also crucial to the search-engines – they have to find your keyword frequency, placement, and prominence, in order to index you correctly.
layers	In HTML you can have 'layers' of screens – one behind the other – and switch to showing either (some are hidden and therefore web-crawlers might not see them or regard them as spam!).
Link farms	These are websites that simply contain a list of links in order to improve the page-ranking of websites – they could get you banned from search-engines altogether!

Merchant Account	An Internet account which will process credit cards and allow on-line access. through a URL link.
navigation	The way people get from one page to another on your website – if your website is complicated provide a site-map of links that give access to every page on your site from your home page.
optimisation	The process of making your website pages friendly to search-engines. Many SEO's (Search-Engine Optimisers) are in the business of ramping-up your page-ranking in order to make your site more popular.
Outbound links	URL Links from your website to other sites.
Page-Rank	(PR) A notional value given by each search-engine in order to rank your site in their search results – this can be affected by a number of factors which are constantly changing and secret to the search-engines involved.
Partial-fulfilment	When you can only supply some of a particular order – the rest has to wait until you get delivery, etc.

Pay Per Click	A means of internet marketing whereby you advertise and only pay when someone clicks on that ad and comes to your site – often you compete with others for keywords.
Paypal	A means of internet credit-transfer – not based on credit card purchase but s person to person transfer of funds.
pdf	A file format (filename.pdf) which is well-known on the internet for downloadable files in printer-friendly format –adobe acrobat.
phishing	A means of scamming the unwary by email – you are invited to click on a link which is false in some way.
proxy-servers	A means of getting onto the internet via another networked route – avoiding intrusion to your computer.
reciprocal links	Linking with another site mutually – they have a link top you in return for your link to them.
robot	See web-crawler
routers	Physical routing devices which give security from hacking intrusion and allow access to the internet, etc.

search-engine	A website and organisation that specialises in providing search facilities to the whole of the web.
search-engine optimisation	SEO – see optimisation
Secure sockets layer	SSL – A ciphered process that is available on some websites – it stops anyone looking at information on that website – often you are told by your browser when you are going onto these sites and a little key symbol is shown at the bottom of your browser whilst on that site - normally much of any website is open to the world!
Shopping trolley	A program that allows you to accumulate your web shopping and pay for it by credit card. In America it is called a shopping cart.
spam	Either repitition of keywords to upgrade your search-engine ranking or unsolicited email.
spiders	See web-crawler
spyware	This is typically cookies which latch onto you when you surf the web. You can get anti-spyware or many of the search-engine taskbars will take care of these annoying intrusions.

submitting	When you have created your website pages and transferred them to your ISP you can submit you website details to the search-engines so that they can index you and allow people to find you.
tables	Tables are used in web pages to separate items – the table's HTML coding can become complicated for the web-crawlers to follow.
tags	HTML codes are known as tags.
title	The HTML title of your page should be as descriptive as possible – it should contain the main keywords for that page and is crucial to the search-engine in indexing your site.
URL	Universal Resource Locator – Yeah right – it's a link to something - OK. It's the address in your web-browser that begins http://whatever.
virus	The web has the unfortunate problem of clever-dicks writing programs to screw your computer in some way – sad but true! Some are Trojan horses which get into your computer and are then activated later – they also screw you!

Web-crawler An automatic program that 'crawls' from one website to another across the web and indexes the website so that others can find you.(also known as robots, bots, spiders, et.al!.)

All titles, listed below, in the Straightforward Guides Series can be purchased online, using credit card or other forms of payment by going to www.straightfowardco.co.uk A discount of 25% per title is offered with online purchases.

Law
A Straightforward Guide to:
Consumer Rights
Bankruptcy Insolvency and the Law
Employment Law
Private Tenants Rights
Family law
Small Claims in the County Court
Contract law
Intellectual Property and the law
Divorce and the law
Leaseholders Rights
The Process of Conveyancing
Knowing Your Rights and Using the Courts
Producing Your own Will
Housing Rights
The Bailiff the law and You
Probate and The Law
Company law
What to Expect When You Go to Court
Guide to Competition Law
Give me Your Money-Guide to Effective Debt Collection
Caring for a Disabled Child

General titles
Letting Property for Profit
Buying, Selling and Renting property
Buying a Home in England and France
Bookkeeping and Accounts for Small Business

Creative Writing
Freelance Writing
Writing Your own Life Story
Writing performance Poetry
Writing Romantic Fiction
Speech Writing

Teaching Your Child to Read and write
Teaching Your Child to Swim
Raising a Child-The Early Years

Creating a Successful Commercial Website
The Straightforward Business Plan
The Straightforward C.V.
Successful Public Speaking

Handling Bereavement
Play the Game-A Compendium of Rules
Individual and Personal Finance
Understanding Mental Illness
The Two Minute Message
Guide to Self Defence
Buying a Used Car
Tiling for Beginners

Go to:

www.straightforwardco.co.uk